GIVING MY SILENCE A VOICE

Giving My Silence a Voice

By Elanena White

Unless otherwise noted, scriptures are taken from the New King James Version and New International Version.
This book should not be used to treat Bipolar Disorder or any other mental illness. I recommend seeking advice from a counselor or medical professional.
National Suicide Prevention Lifeline 1-800-273-TALK (8255).
suicidepreventionlifeline.org

Rape, Abuse & Incest National Network
The Rape, Abuse & Incest National Network (RAINN) is the nation's largest anti-sexual assault organization. Among its programs, RAINN created and operates the National Sexual Assault Hotline at 1.800.656.HOPE and the National Sexual Assault Online Hotline at rainn.org. This nationwide partnership of more than 1,100 local rape crisis centers provides victims of sexual assault with free, confidential services, 24 hours per day, and 7 days per week. These hotlines have helped over 1.3 million people since RAINN's founding in 1994.
NAMI National Alliance on Mental Illness Help Line
1-800-950-NAMI (6264) or info@nami.org
The NAMI Help Line can be reached Monday through Friday, 10 am–6 pm, ET.

Help Line staff and volunteers are prepared to answer your questions about mental health issues

Acknowledgments

I would first like to thank my Lord and Savior Jesus Christ. Without him I am nothing. I thank God for every gift he has bestowed upon me. I thank God for allowing me to minister to people through my books so that they may know you are never so deep in sin that God cannot use you. To the love of my life, my friend, and my soul mate Eddie James White, the first one to read my books and listen as I ramble on and on. I love you and God hasn't brought us this far to leave us. My four beautiful children MaiKeyah Romby, Aushantia Clary, Jameyah Cole, and Knolej White the reasons that I breathe.
To my mommy Betty Adams Leaks I thank you for being my biggest supporter and
My strength. For every word you spoke over my life I pray God shows you favor. You taught me how to be a good mother, wife, and what it takes to be a true woman of God. Shirley White for coming to the rescue when I needed you and for being a great supporter
To my siblings Isaac, Jason, Isaiah, and Keisha McMullin, and I love y'all.

Jason and Isaac for giving me the advice to make my books successful.

Prophetess Brenda Jerro (My Prayer Warrior) thank you for always being there when I question myself and what God has for me. I love you.

My Pastor's Larry D. Yarbrough and First Lady Shaneil "PJ" Yarbrough I thank God for bringing you 2 into my life. You will never know what your prayers and words of encouragement mean to me. I love y'all from the bottom of my heart.

Stephanie Gates, Keidra Williams, Ruthie Love, Dalesha Manning, Ginger Williams (My Sisters, I love y'all to life)Mashell Marshall, my ride or die. I love you hunti!!! Cynthia Williams, Margie (Sweetie) Owens, Mary Crosby (who keeps my walk with Jesus straight), Emma Wofford (my encourager) J2W (Jonathan Wofford) I love you my brother in Christ you always encouraging me to do what God says and always finding a way to help me. It means a lot to me. I would not be a good business woman without this group of people in my life. They taught and teach me everything. Deanna and Grady Tracy, Captain Donnie Marvels, Michael Thomason, Michael Bradshaw, Clarence Thrower, and John Wesley O'Hara. I thank God for each one of you being in my life.

To all my readers God Bless!!!!!!!!!!

This book is dedicated to my mommy because no matter what storm I was in or going through, she is always there to hold my hand through it. Even when I didn't want to write this book because I was shame and worried what others would think or say, she encouraged me until I finished writing. God truly blessed me when he gave me her as a mother.

"For I know the plans I have for you," declares the LORD, "plans to prosper you and not to harm you, plans to give you hope and a future. Then you will call on me and come and pray to me, and I will listen to you." (Jeremiah 29:11-12, NIV)

Prologue

She walks with her head held high with such grace. When she smiles it lights up a room. She never ever holds herself above anyone else, though at times it appears she is. Although she never apologizes she is apathetic. She remains firm in thought and mind. She does what she does and is meant to do; whether others approve or not; during which time her head is always held high. When she disagrees she never rants, but states her case; knowing beforehand some will accept others won't; feeling at peace that she has done so. She never ever compares herself to others; that's not important; she already knows she's a part of the world because she is alive. She works with life's difficulties with a clear and focused mind and when the chips are down she picks them up one by one; being wise to weep when needed, laugh when needed and become angry when needed; in other words she accepts all those things and never denies them. She is the first and foremost to blame herself for her difficulties; with the knowledge that she, too, was a contributor; no matter how the dice are tossed. Behind the mask of her life are issues that are leading her on a downward spiral. It has been said, "Depression is a cry in the soul that something is missing." And many, many women experience that cry at one time or another to one degree or another. I bet no one knows she lives with a mental illness called Bi-Polar Disorder. She has finally decided she cannot deal with this on her own and she will "Give Her Silence a Voice".......

My Life

Married for twelve years, four beautiful children, successful career, wonderful church life, beautiful home, nice car, an ok bank account, and vacations once a year. You think I have it together and a perfect life. You thought? On the outside looking in yes all that seems to be true. You would never think behind the million dollar smile there was sadness. You would never think behind the makeup there is fear of what the future holds. You would never think underneath the fancy clothing and handbags lies insecurities, hidden secrets that have not been revealed or even dealt with. I know longer looked forward to each new day, I hated to even wake up. I had lost the desire to be with my husband. I lost my desire to lay on the couch and watch movies with my children. I used to love talking to my girls, telling them stories and listening to their chatter, but even the sound of their voices had become irritating. I no longer wanted to talk, to listen, or to answer anyone's questions. I just wanted to be alone. None of my previous hobbies or activities interested me anymore. I didn't want to leave the house, or my bed. All I wanted to do was sleep, eternally, if possible. Was I going through a midlife crisis?

In the brain of this supposed to be so brilliant,

sanctified and filled with the Holy Ghost lies suicidal thoughts numerous times a day. How can you go to church for Wednesday night prayer and bible study, church on Sunday to get a word from the Lord trying to praise your way through a storm that is about to come full circle you ask. It's simple I'm good at putting on a front that everything is ok. I don't need everyone in my business gossiping and assuming what's going on in my supposed to be perfect life. I pray and fast, I pray and fast, God is not listening to me. So I thought or did I just not trust him? Am I in my own way? I am finally ready to let the world know that I live with a mental illness called Bi-Polar

Disorder. I am no longer ashamed or worried about what others will say. This is my story of how I gave my silence a voice finally.

How Did I Get Here Again?

Walking down the long hospital corridor, I sensed that with each step I took, I was losing a piece of myself. As I passed through the door at the end of the hallway, I knew my life would never be the same. I felt defeated and confused. What's someone like me doing in a place like this again? I wondered. It was my first admission to a hospital mental hospital since I was young girl. Somewhere in my mind I never expected to be here again. It seemed that I had everything to live for, but my mind was consumed with thoughts of death. At the age of 36 what could have snapped in my mind that would land me flat on my back on antidepressants once again. Once again fighting with the demons of my past. Once again letting this Bi-Polar Disorder take over my life. I thought if I stayed close to God I would no longer have to deal with this again. How did I let Satan sneak up on me like this again? Does this make me less of a Christian? Has God closed his ears to me? These are questions I needed answers to that I asked myself everyday now. I longed for a peace of mind, I longed for joy, and I longed to be delivered from my past of hurt and pain. Lord knows I have been to enough healing and delivering church services. Did I not except my healing?

Early Years

I was born in a small town where everybody knew everybody. My mom was 15 at the time of my birth and married at 14 to my dad who was 10 years her junior. Weird I know but in that time it was very common to be married at such a young age. Plus you don't even know her story. It is not a very pleasant one, that's a whole book by itself. From the moment I was in my mother's womb she said she dedicated me to God. I took my first step in the church. Wouldn't walk for my mother but I did for my great aunt who just happened to be a preacher. I have been stubborn and hardheaded all my life. Could that be a part of my life's problem? Probably.

My childhood was a rollercoaster. My mom left my dad after ten years of marriage. We moved to a new town to get away from my dad's many demons that plagued our family. I and my brothers were always picked on by our neighboring cousins for the things that my dad had done. I personally was glad my mom took us and moved. When we first left we stayed in a women's crisis center until a husband and family took us in. They were nice people on the outside to others but were very deceptive and manipulative people. They tried to turn me against my very own mother. How could you tell a child your mom doesn't want you? When clearly she showed me different. It got so bad we had to move and it started a chain of events that would cause my life to never be the same again.

The Incident That Changed My Life

How could someone that you trust hurt you in a way that it will have you questioning your very existence? At the age of nine I was raped over a period of time by someone who was in the family. No blood relation. What a man would want with a nine year old child I have no idea. He was a sick man because not only did he do it to me but to other young girls. To keep me from telling my mom he played on my emotions by telling me he would kill my mother, me, and my brothers. As I sit and write this I for the life of me cannot remember where my brothers was when this would take place. My mom would be at work. I can still smell the baby oil (I hate the smell right today) that he would use to make what he was doing easier. He even used a condom. This sick man even had the nerve to be gentle as I cannot remember feeling any pain. I do however remember crying and praying to God that my mom would come home each time. I would close my eyes and try to think of being somewhere pleasant so his time on me would hurry up and pass. I can remember taking a bath afterwards and asking God why. What did I do to deserve this? The killing part about all of this after he violated me he treated me horribly. My mom would always have dinner cooked before she left for work, but he would be the one to feed us. He would not let me eat. I went to bed hungry many nights. Why didn't I tell my mom you asked? I didn't tell because not only was he a pedophile, he was also a crazed woman beater. When he told me he would kill my mother, me and my brothers I believed him. His sexual abuse went on for months. I hated his guts. Every time he touched me that hate grew stronger. The hate was so strong many nights I plotted on how to stab him and kill him. It was a couple of times when he raped me I tried so hard to fight him off me, but I was just no match for him. He would hit me in the top of my head so bruises wouldn't show. A nine year old going through this trauma and no one could see through the pain I was in. In my mind not even God. I always felt dirty and just walking as a shell of myself. I often wondered why no counselor or teacher could see the signs of a broken abused child. After the first time I was violated I withdrew from my friends and stayed to myself. I never told a single person what was happening to me.

One night my rapist started a fight with my mom and I mean it was bad one. This time my mom got the best of him and he left. I finally got the courage to tell her what he had been doing to me. I remember seeing the hurt in her eyes. She held me and told me she believed me. No one will never know the relief I felt when she told me she believed me. But guess what that fool came back. I thought my mom was going to pack us up and leave. Nope that's not what happened right then. At the time I thought my mom was scared to leave, not knowing that she had contacted a friend who was a social worker. The social worker told her that if she left right then and reported what happened she could possibly go to jail too. I can't remember the exact details but I do remember she got me and my brothers away, my rapist did go to jail, but so did my mom too just like the social worker said she would. While my rapist and mom was locked up my brothers and I were put into two separate foster homes. My mom did eventually get out after it was determined she had no idea what my rapist was doing to me. Though they knew she was innocence they still felt it was her fault for me being put in that situation. My brothers and I did not get to go home with my mom right away. The foster parents we each had were physically, mentally, and emotionally abusive. It just seemed like my family could not catch a break. The state took us from my mom because they felt like she was negligent, yet they put us in homes were the foster parents only took kids in for a check. We barely got meals and got no sympathy. I never knew people could be so cold hearted. I was eventually taken out of my foster home and placed in another. All the while this was going on my mom fought to get her children back and she eventually did. My rapist got a jail sentence but he eventually got out. When I got older my mom found out he had the audacity to be a mentor to children. Of course she put a stop to that. My question is how he even got a chance to be a mentor when he is a registered sex offender. When we were finally reunited with my mother we were some broken children. For myself I never got over the idea I was worthy of love. I hid what happened to me in the deep corners of my mind. I would not allow myself to even think about it. This started a cycle of hate, hostility, resentment, and questioning people's motives. My mom went beyond the call of duty to prove that she loved me and my brothers. She never let us out of her sight. I personally believe after all we been through she started running background checks on who ever she left us with while she worked. We finally settled into being a family again. My mom would take us to the park and read us stories. One of my fondest memories of me and my mom is when she would braid or even comb my hair she would always give me a mirror and say momma's pretty girl. I never wanted a hair out of place. I never lost a bead or a hair bow. Even though my mom told me constantly I was a pretty girl I still felt so ugly on the inside. I never properly dealt with everything I had been through and I was a ticking time bomb.

A Troubled Teen

All that I endured as an adolescence began to come out in my actions as I arrived at my teen years. The truth of the matter is I hated myself and everyone that was around me. I felt like everyone loved my brothers more than me. No one treated me that way it was just a trick of the enemy. I cursed out teachers and fought my peers, I had so much undealt with anger in me I just unleashed on any and everyone except my mother. I remember her telling me there is nothing wrong with you and you can control your mouth because you have never cursed me out. She just didn't know I feared her like no other, but she was the only one.

This time in my life we were living in a nice trailer park. There were a lot of children that stayed in the trailer park too. There was one particular family that lived out there and their children were the bullies of the trailer park. It was two boys and one girl who was the youngest. I was a couple years older than the girl but that didn't stop her from picking. Normally I ignored her but this particular time I had a bad day and I was just not having it. It was raining that day so I had a long umbrella I was carrying. I can't even remember what she was saying to me. I kept telling her to leave me alone. She messed around and pushed me off the bus. I went to work with my umbrella beating her and her brothers with it. I just kept hitting until I tore my umbrella up. I don't remember who stopped the beating. I beat all three of them so bad their mom called the police on me. I didn't go to jail but I had to go to court. In the court room I tried to explain the girl and her brothers had been bullying me and other kids. The judge believed me because they had been to court a time or two. I got chastised because the bruises they had from me beating them looked like a deranged lunatic had gotten a hold to them. I was sentenced to take anger management classes. I'm just going to be honest those classes did me no good because I felt like I shouldn't be there. I faked and did what I had to do to get a good report to the judge so I could graduate from anger management. I had everyone fooled but my mom. My anger finally had gotten uncontrollable to the point I tried to fight my teachers. I always felt like I was in the right for defending myself against what I thought the teachers were doing to me, The school recommended to my mother that I go to a mental institution because something mental had to be going on with me. She followed their advice and had me put in.

Pinewood Mental Hospital

Let me just start by saying if you are not mental when you go in you will be when you come out. They diagnosed me with Schizophrenia, Depression, and Bi-Polar Disorder. I was on so many different medications. Before the medicine got into my system I took everything for a joke. I would go to the group meetings and they would ask each one of us "how you feel today" my response would be "I don't." I know I was one of the ones who had one of the worse attitudes. I had so much going on in my mind, in my life I just didn't know how to deal and I just didn't care. Truth of the matter I didn't care if I lived or died. A sad way for a child to feel but I did. I had given up on myself and had lost all hope. The many medicines I was on (Prozac, Lithium, and a bunch of other stuff I couldn't pronounce) finally made its way in my system. I can't really remember much but I do know I was a walking zombie. It was like I was in another body. I couldn't even remember my name. I cried all the time and tried to commit suicide numerous times. My mom would come see me and I would tell them I had no mother. Not because I didn't want to see her but because the medicine had I so messed up I really didn't remember her. At the time my mom was coming the state was paying for my stay so if I said I didn't want to see her they wouldn't let her see me. The truth was they were trying to hide how drugged up they had me. My mom had come every weekend to see me and they wouldn't let her even get a glimpse of me. She finally had enough and began to pay my medical bills herself on her insurance. The very next time she came to see me they tried to deny her until she informed them she was paying the bill and they better let her see me. My doctor brought me to her. I was so drugged out I didn't know who she was. My grandmother was with her and she demanded to list of medication I was on. When they saw the list of medicines I was on they through a fit. My grandmother knew all about the medicines I was on. She knew the dosage was too high. My doctor reduced the dosage and I slowly came back to myself. After about maybe 9 months of treatment and going to group meetings I was finally able to leave only to return 2 more times before I finally got all my demons and things of my past to lie dormant. That period in my life is kind of dim due to the different medicines I was taking. I was probably around 14 years old. Can you imagine being that age and dealing with mental illness? Even when I got out I still felt like no one understood me. I have always been kind of weird and had my own sense of style. I was finally able to deal with things and life better without taking medication. Don't get me wrong I had my up days and down days but I learned how to cope with it. I learned to get by myself and think of the good things about my life.

Someone Who I Know Loves Me

At the age of 16 I got pregnant with my first child. The father and I were no longer together but we were great friends and he was very supportive. My mom was an angel on earth. She didn't approve of me being pregnant out of wedlock but she did not turn her back on me. She encouraged me to keep on with my education and whatever my career choice was she would help me in every way possible. During this time I was going to a Baptist church that my baby father was also member of. Being a member of this church almost sent me back into depression. Because my baby father and I was having a baby out of wedlock they made us get in front of the church and ask for forgiveness from God and from them. Now I knew all the secrets of the church from the pulpit on down to the congregation. I knew about several of the teenage girls having abortions and they never had to get up there and ask for forgiveness. I felt shame and like I was being ridiculed. I had worked so hard to keep my anger hidden and now I was being embarrassed literally in front of God and everybody. After that incident, my family and I left that church. No one wants to go to church and feel judged. What happened to me did affect my way of viewing my sins and being in church while I was sinning. I also never really trusted church folks again until I got grown and learned what they did to me was wrong. I gave birth to a 5 pound little girl. The minute she was born changed my whole outlook on life. Now there were periods when I couldn't deal with her crying and just being nervous as a young mother. I thank God because my mom was there every step of the way. Having my little girl helped me to deal with my mental illness a whole lot better and made me want to strive for greatness. Everything I did that was successful I did for my baby girl. I finally thought my life was headed on the right track until tragedy struck me and my brothers.

A Part of Me Gone

When my baby girl was about 9 months old my father died. He did get to hold his first grandbaby before he passed, but he never got to see her beauty because he was blind. Losing my dad played a big part of how I lived my life in the world and also played a part of my mental illness as an adult. The weekend he died he begged for me to come with my brothers and spend the weekend with him. I wouldn't go because he stayed in the woods and I wanted to be with my friends. The guilt I felt for not going and spending that weekend has haunted me until this day. My dad was not always there for us and even acted like he didn't care but I still loved him. I never thought that I would get older and not have my daddy still here. A piece of me still longs for him. I sometimes wish I could call him and ask "daddy why my husband does some of the things he does." I also feel like my daddy robbed me of being a "daddy's girl." I used to date men a few years older than me and I really believe I was looking for the characteristics of my daddy in these men. Now that I think about it my husband has a lot of his characteristics.

The death of my father was another hole in my belt of depression because I really didn't know how to deal with it.

Senior Year

My senior year of high school was one of the most exciting times of my life. It was exciting to me because in spite of all my obstacles I had made it to the finish line. When it came time for homecoming no one could be more excited than me. That year I didn't have a date and chose to be with my friends. One of my classmates and a member of my church had been had a crush on me but I would never give him the time of day. He just wasn't my type but he was cool as a friend. He told me he needed to talk to me about something and asked me to walk with him outside of the game. It was the biggest mistake of my life and woke up my hatred for men all over again. He raped me over and over and over again. It was as if he was punishing me for not wanting to date him. I will never forget laying in the woods, because that's where he forced me to go, with his fluids all over me. I cried until my throat was sore. He left me in the woods like nothing ever happened. I never told a soul what happened to me. Not even my best friend who I told everything. I remember getting off the ground and I could hardly walk because he was so rough. I dusted myself off as best I could and tried to get my hair together as best I could. I called my stepdad to come get me. He could kind of tell something was wrong but he never said anything. I didn't report what happened to me because the boy father was the pastor of my church. I did not want to hurt his mom or be ridiculed once again. I just really also thought no one would believe me. I didn't want to be the talk of the school or town. So I did what I do best act like nothing ever happened. This day as I am writing is the first time I have ever spoken about what happened. That night when I got home I took a lot of Tylenol hoping I would not wake up. I know I had my little girl to live for. I couldn't understand what it was about me that made men want to hurt me. I kept my silence but I was slowly dying inside. Of course taking all those Tylenol didn't kill me obviously but it should have. I asked God what he was keeping me here for. At the time I didn't understand but I most certainly do now. I had to go through this so I could help someone else. I can't tell a drug addict how to recover or deal with it if I have never done it. I can tell young girls, teenagers, and women my story about being raped and how I should have told somebody so it wouldn't be another hole in my belt for depression. These issues I had when I was a child and a teenager I thought would never surface back up in my life but they have. The devil thought he would use these to destroy me and cause me to go on and commit suicide.

Adult Life Struggling to Survive

The different incidents and tragedies of my past I thought I had dealt with helped mold my mental illness as they laid dormant waiting to come to the surface. I now know that the only way to end the stigma of being Bi-Polar and depressed is to be loud and proud about who I am. Make it known that I am here and I am not dangerous or broken, different yes, but no less worthy of love and respect than anyone else. I have made friends with my Bipolar Disorder, it has been a road to this point, but I now find myself grateful for and even proud of it. It has had a major role in shaping who I am, and I like who I am and so do so many others.

Life Marches On

The depression part of my mental illness is a strange illness. Most terminally ill people have a spirit that longs to live, even though the body is dying. As a depressed person, I felt that my spirit had already died, my body just refused to follow it to the grave. I was torn between my desire to end my own suffering and the knowledge that in so doing I would be leaving a legacy of incredible pain and sorrow for my kids and my husband. My family had no idea I was struggling with depression and being Bi-Polar silently. All they knew was one day I'm happy and floating on clouds and one day I'm irritable and a crying mess. I had been dealing with this silently for a couple of years. It was as though tiny bandages had been placed on a large, gaping wound, but it continued to bleed and would not heal. I prayed that God would restore my joy and peace with in him but how he can restore when I haven't truthfully dealt with the hurt and pain of the past. I deemed myself a failure as a wife, a mother, and a Christian. My doctor had given me excellent medical treatment over the years, but I began to realize that while those in the mental health profession had done all they could to treat my body and mind (by treating my brain chemistry and emotions), a key element of my being had never really been considered: my spirit. . My doctor had prescribed me this medicine that helped control my moods but what about the brokenness that I felt in my heart.

A Change in My Spirit

My husband took the first step in his life by joining a church we both loved and I joined him. Watching my husband surrender to God did something to my spirit too. We started praying together and doing devotions together and in doing so I could feel a little of my brokenness leave every time we would pray. I made a vision board with nothing but bible scriptures to remind me of the love God has for me. I also prayed and asked God to truly deliver me from every hurt, grudge, pity party, self-doubt and anything that was not like him.

The Beauty of God

When I allowed God to deliver me and not man he opened my eyes to a whole other level of mental illness and where it comes from. I learned that the roots of my depression were not emotional, as I had assumed, but spiritual. I discovered many lies I had believed my entire life, which greatly affected my personality and influenced the way I had chosen to live. One of the most destructive untruths I learned about myself was that I was not good enough. As a young child I began to feel that I was somehow flawed, substandard, and inferior because of everything that had happened to me that I had no control of. I lived my life being people pleasers trying to prevent others from discovering how worthless I thought I was. Causing anger to fester inside of me instead of being myself. I lacked a healthy sense of my own value, I became dependent on the approval of those around me to make me feel good about myself, earning their praise through trying to be the best at everything, and trying to be perfect. It became a costly addiction to my spirit, mind and soul. It got to a point where I couldn't do it no more and something had to give. I had to allow God to come in and minister to me through the Holy Spirit. The Holy Spirit had to speak to my wounded, brokenhearted, and weary soul. All those time I was running to healing and deliverance services I could not be healed and delivered because I was trusting for a touch from man to do it instead of allowing the spirit of God to do it. Not saying the men of God was false but I was up there trusting the wrong thing which was hindering my healing. When I allowed God to do the work he let me know I was beautifully and wonderfully made and created in his image. My work was of no consequence and my achievements did not matter. What I did or did not do did not determine my worth but who I belonged to did. I was a beloved daughter of the King of

Kings! Knowing this truth would transform my whole mindset. No longer would I have to strive for the approval of others. God's opinion of me was all that mattered, and I only accepted what he had to say. All this time no matter what I been through, no matter what sin I had committed, God loved me just the way I was. I was free to discover His purpose for my life.

Before having this encounter with God and the Holy Spirit, I had lost almost lost my mind and all hope of ever getting my joy and peace. I thought I would live with being Bi-Polar and depressed for the rest of my life. But God whispered to me "I have plans for you, my child and it's a future full of hope!" He promised, "When you seek me with all your heart I will bring you back from captivity" (Jeremiah 29:13-14). Won't he do it? I'm a living witness he will. I began to seek him continuously by studying his Word, listening to His voice, and praying. God fulfilled His promise. I no longer live with depression or consider myself Bi-Polar. I no longer take medication to control my moods but I look to the hills where all my help comes. I trust and look to God for every area of my life because he is my strong tower.

New Life

I never would have chosen to be labeled or diagnosed as Bi-Polar. Also depression is not something that I would have chosen for myself, I am now grateful for the blessings I reaped because of it: an understanding of my true identity and worth, an intimate relationship with God, and a strong faith in Him to encourage and minister to someone else. Willard Thiessen once stated, "Sometimes what looks to us like destruction is actually what God will use for our absolute deliverance." I believe that. For so long I was ashamed and feared what people would think if they knew what I was living with especially being in the church. Even as I write this book I can feel the presence of God with me and I no longer want to cry or hide my face in shame. It took my husband giving himself to God for me to truly deal with the demons of my past and for me to seek God in spirit and in truth. My perspective on being brokenhearted has changed. While unpleasant, I know that pain serves a purpose in the life of a Christian. I am also keenly aware that while our difficulties may seem unbearable at times, there is nothing that God cannot do, and nothing He cannot use for our good. I am grateful that God gave me the tools to finally give my silence a voice.

Psalm 43

Psalm 43, the psalmist asks, "Why are you downcast, O my soul? Why so disturbed within me?" Maybe you're asking similar questions today. If you are, I want you to know that you are not alone. There is light at the end of the dark tunnel you may be in right now. It has been said, "Depression is a cry in the soul that something is missing." And many, many women experience that cry at one time or another to one degree or another. Maybe you're experiencing it today.

Our lives are full of emotional ups and downs. Almost all of us experience the "blues" from time to time. And did you know that nearly every woman, at some time in her life, will experience a mild to serious form of depression that might even be incapacitating…. "The pace of life, chronic stress, relationship conflicts, hurts, rejections, and the ups and downs of the immune system all wreak havoc with our moods." On top of this, our female bodies are constantly adjusting to hormonal fluctuations. There is no simple explanation for depression. It is complex, interrelated and affects the whole body and person. There is some comfort though in knowing that depression is so common. Anyone can experience it, but it is more common in women than men. And we as Christians are not immune.

A Downcast Soul

If your soul is downcast today think of it this way: "God has designed us with the capacity for experiencing depression." If God created us with this capacity then surely He understands when we experience it. Maybe depression is like pain. Pain is good when it's a signal for danger; it's bad when it rages out of control. Likewise, depression is a normal reaction to many things we experience, but when it spirals out of control it can be destructive. If you are feeling depressed there is hope. First of all, depression is treatable. Don't be afraid to seek help from your doctor or a Christian counselor. Tell someone how you're feeling. But most importantly, I want to assure you that God; your creator and Heavenly Father understands your depression. Don't be reluctant to go to God with your feelings and questions. That's what the psalmist is doing in Psalm 43. He is brutally honest with God. He asks the hard questions. And he ends by putting his hope in Almighty God.

According to Dr. Catherine Hart Weber, "every fourth woman around you has the potential for becoming seriously depressed…" If you are that woman you know there are no simple answers for the questions you may be asking today. But that doesn't mean there are no answers at all. Sometimes just understanding gives relief. To help you understand what might be behind your depression here are six possible causes of depression based on Psalm 107.

The first is DISCOURAGEMENT. The psalmist explains that when we wander in desert wastelands so hungry and thirsty that it feels like life is ebbing away or we just can't find our way and are constantly unsettled, discouragement set in and often leads to depression.

Another possible cause of depression is SPIRITUAL DARKNESS. Darkness and gloom, bitterness and distress (all forms of depression) are the outcomes if we've rebelled against the Word of God and despised His counsel.

The third cause of depression found in Psalm 107 is SINFUL DISOBEDIENCE. When we are out and out sinful, acting out our rebellious ways, our disobedience invariably leads to depression.

The fourth possible cause is simply the OVERWHELMING WAVES of life. Often we are just going about our business, even enjoying the Lord, when the ups and downs of our experiences take us to the extremes emotionally. The fifth cause of depression is SPIRITUAL DROUGHT. There are times when the rivers and flowing springs of our soul dry up. We don't always know what's behind these times, but prolonged drought can bring on depression.

The last possible cause of depression mentioned in Psalm 107 is LOSS. Loss takes many forms....loss of loved ones, of income or security, of health or a particular time period in our life. This decrease that comes our way with loss often brings with it depression.

(Information from Linda Linder 2004-2007)

As you identify the reason behind your depression and you put into action the things you can do, you will discover that the Lord will do His part. He will satisfy and settle you. He will bring you out of darkness and deep gloom. He will rescue you from your distress. He will turn the desert of your soul into pools of water and the parched ground of your raw emotions into flowing springs. He promises.

The Bible and Depression

You won't find the term "depression" in the Bible, except in the New Living Translation. Instead, the Bible uses words such as downcast, sad, forlorn, discouraged, downhearted, mourning, troubled, miserable, despairing, and brokenhearted. You will, however, find many Bible people showing the symptoms of this disease: Hagar, Moses, Naomi, Hannah, Saul, David, Solomon, Elijah, Nehemiah, Job, and Jeremiah, John the Baptist, Judas Iscariot, and Paul. What does the Bible say about depression? What truths can we glean from God's Word about this condition? No one is immune from

Depression.

The Bible shows that depression can strike anyone. Poor people like Naomi, the mother-in-law of Ruth, and very rich people, like King Solomon, suffered from depression. Young people, like David, and older people, like Job, were also afflicted. Depression strikes both men and women, like Hannah, who was barren, and men, like Jeremiah, the "weeping prophet." Understandably, depression can come after a defeat. When David and his men reached Ziklag, they found it destroyed by fire and their wives and sons and daughters taken captive. So David and his men wept aloud until they had no strength left to weep. (1 Samuel 30:3-4, NIV)

Oddly, an emotional letdown can also come after a great victory. Elijah the prophet defeated the false prophets of Baal on Mount Carmel in a stunning display of God's power (1 Kings 18:38). But instead of being encouraged, Elijah, fearing Jezebel's revenge, was weary and afraid. He (Elijah) came to a broom bush, sat down under it and prayed that he might die. "I have had enough, LORD," he said. "Take my life; I am no better than my ancestors." Then he lay down under the bush and fell asleep. (1 Kings 19:4-5, NIV)

God Is Not Angry About Our Depression

Discouragement and depression are normal parts of being human. They can be triggered by the death of a loved one, illness, loss of a job or status, divorce, leaving home, or many other traumatic events. The Bible does not show God punishing his people for their sadness. Rather, he acts as a loving Father: (Zavada, 2015)

David was greatly distressed because the men were talking of stoning him; each one was bitter in spirit because of his sons and daughters. But David found strength in the LORD his God. (1 Samuel 30:6, NIV)

Elkanah made love to his wife Hannah, and the LORD remembered her. So in the course of time Hannah became pregnant and gave birth to a son. She named him Samuel, saying, "Because I asked the LORD for him." (1 Samuel 1:19-20, NIV)

For when we came into Macedonia, we had no rest, but we were harassed at every turn—conflicts on the outside, fears within. But God, who comforts the downcast, comforted us by the coming of Titus, and not only by his coming but also by the comfort you had given him. (2 Corinthians 7:5-7, NIV)

God Is Our Hope in the Midst of Depression

One of the great truths of the Bible is that God is our hope when we are in trouble, including depression. The message is clear. When depression hits, fix your eyes on God, his power, and his love for you:

The LORD himself goes before you and will be with you; he will never leave you nor forsake you. Do not be afraid; do not be discouraged. (Deuteronomy 31:8, NIV)

Have I not commanded you? Be strong and courageous. Do not be afraid; do not be discouraged, for the LORD your God will be with you wherever you go. (Joshua 1:9, NIV)

The LORD is close to the brokenhearted and saves those who are crushed in spirit. (Psalm 34:18, NIV) So do not fear, for I am with you; do not be dismayed, for I am your God. I will strengthen you and help you; I will uphold you with my righteous right hand. (Isaiah 41:10, NIV)

"For I know the plans I have for you," declares the LORD, "plans to prosper you and not to harm you, plans to give you hope and a future. Then you will call on me and come and pray to me, and I will listen to you." (Jeremiah 29:11-12, NIV)

And I will pray the Father, and he shall give you another Comforter, that he may abide with you forever; (John 14:16, KJV)

(Jesus said) "And surely I am with you always, to the very end of the age." (Matthew 28:20, NIV)

For we live by faith, not by sight. (2 Corinthians, 5:7, NIV)

From the desk of Elanena White

This book is special to me because this is my story. We as people do not realize how mental illness affects our communities as well as people in the church. We walk around like we have it altogether when our spirit is crying out help me. It is my hope that this book blesses somebody. May the spirit of God rest on you.

Made in the USA
Coppell, TX
03 September 2024

36772043R00046